Deep Freeze

PIONEER EDITION

By Sandra Markle

CONTENTS

LIFE IN A DEEP
IN A DEEP
Freeze

How do animals survive the Arctic's c-c-cold winters?

BY SANDRA MARKLE

A Cool Crowd. *Walruses spend most of their time in water. Yet they rest and have babies on huge chunks of floating ice.*

S now and ice cover the ground. Strong winds blow. The air is freezing cold. It is winter in the Arctic.

Where is the Arctic? Look at the map. The Arctic is all the land and water inside the red circle. It includes the North Pole.

The Arctic is always cold. Its **tundra,** or flat land, stays frozen all year. Yet many animals live here. They have ways to stay warm—and alive.

Snow Baby. *Most grizzly bear cubs are born while their mothers hibernate.*

Big Teeth. *Walruses grow long tusks, or teeth. Some are 30 inches long!*

Sleepy Winters

Some animals are not bothered by the cold. They sleep all winter. That is what grizzly bears do.

Grizzly Bear The grizzly bear eats a lot in spring, summer, and fall. It gets fat. Then winter comes. The grizzly bear **hibernates,** or sleeps deeply. The bear does not eat again until spring. It lives off its stored fat.

WORDWISE

blubber: thick layer of fat under the skin

hibernate: to sleep deeply for months

tundra: flat area without trees where the ground stays frozen all year

The Layered Look

In winter, the Arctic Ocean is covered with ice. Yet some animals hunt in the water. Fat keeps them warm.

Walrus This animal spends most of its time in cold ocean water. It dives to the ocean floor. It digs for clams.

How does a walrus stay warm? It has a thick layer of **blubber,** or fat. The fat holds in heat.

Harp Seal Harp seals also have a layer of blubber. The blubber helps them stay warm in icy water.

Harp seals are expert swimmers. They are fast in the water. They race after fish. They can stay underwater for 30 minutes at a time. Without their blubber, they would freeze!

Safety in Numbers. *Muskoxen live in groups. They form a line when danger is near. This helps them stay safe.*

Dressed for Winter

In winter, many Arctic animals grow a thick coat, or layer of fur. The coats keep them safe and warm.

Muskox The muskox is always covered with shaggy hair. In winter, woolly fur grows under the shaggy hair. This thick fur coat keeps the muskox warm.

Arctic Fox The arctic fox changes color with the seasons. In summer, it has brown fur. In winter, it grows white fur. Its white coat lets the fox blend in with the snow. This helps the fox stay safe from hungry animals.

Snowy owl

Wearing White

Some animals do not change color in winter. They wear white all year. Their color helps them hide in the snow.

Arctic Hare Some arctic hares live in the far north. The snow never melts. These hares have white fur all year. This keeps them safe. Hungry animals have a hard time seeing them.

Snowy Owl Snowy owls are white birds. They blend in with the snow. These birds have two layers of feathers. The thick feathers keep them warm.

5

Suited for the

Arctic animals have fur or feathers to keep warm in winter. People are not so lucky. We have to wear thick layers of clothes. Compare how people and polar bears stay warm in the Arctic.

BODY A 4-inch layer of fat keeps in body heat.

EAR Small ears prevent heat loss.

FUR Stiff, oily outer hairs shed water. Woolly undercoat traps body heat.

NOSE A keen sense of smell finds food even in the dark.

PAWS Curved claws help the bear climb and dig in the ice. Rough pads keep the bear from slipping. Thick fur keeps the bear's feet warm.

Cold

HAT A thick hat holds in heat given off by the head.

EAR FLAPS Ear flaps block wind and keep ears warm.

COAT This thick coat traps body heat. It keeps out the cold.

GLOVES Thick gloves keep hands from freezing in very cold weather.

BOOTS Snow boots have deep ridges on the bottom. They help people walk across snow and ice.

PANTS Snow pants are waterproof to keep legs dry and warm.

People of the

Many animals live in the Arctic. They have fat and fur to stay warm. People also live in the Arctic. How do they survive?

Arctic people wear thick clothes. They build warm homes. They work hard to live in the bitter cold.

Arctic life has changed over time. But people have always found ways to survive.

Arctic Hunters

Living in the Arctic has never been easy. The ground is frozen. It is too cold for plants. So people cannot grow food. What do they eat?

Long ago, Arctic people ate only meat. They hunted seals, whales, walruses, and caribou. These meals were packed with fat. Food like this helped the hunters stay warm.

Homes of Skin. *In summer, people lived in tents that they could move. The tents were made of animal skin.*

Arctic

All From Animals

Hunting gave people more than food. It also gave them clothes, homes, and tools. Arctic people used animals for almost everything!

People made clothes from animal skins. They made needles and other tools from bone. They even made sleds and boats from animal skins and bone.

Homes on the Go

People in the Arctic were nomads. That means they moved from place to place. People took their homes with them.

In winter, people made igloos. These were houses made of snow. In summer, people used tents. The tents were made of animal skins and bones.

In the Past.
Arctic people often traveled in dogsleds (below). A woman carried her baby in a papoose, or backpack (right).

Arctic Travel

Snow and ice were everywhere. How did people get from place to place? They used dogsleds. Dogs pulled the sleds through the snow.

People also built boats. The boats were made of animal skins and bone. People used the boats to hunt in the ocean. They caught fish, whales, and seals.

Changing Times

Today, life is different in the Arctic. Modern tools are changing how people live.

Most people do not wear animal skins. They dress in modern clothes. Most people do not live in tents or igloos. They live in houses. Most people do not use dogsleds. They ride snowmobiles.

Modern Living.
Today, people use snowmobiles to get around (right). Arctic clothing and culture are a mix of old and new (below).

Jobs in the Arctic

These are not the only changes. People have different jobs too. Some work as miners. Others build homes. Some people work for oil companies. Some teach in schools.

Arctic people make money in other ways too. Some give tours. Some take visitors hunting or fishing. Others make art to sell.

A Story of Survival

Today, life in the Arctic is still hard. Winters are long. The weather is freezing cold. The snow and ice are deep.

Arctic people face many dangers. Yet they are tough. They find ways to survive. They prove you don't have to be a polar bear to live in the Arctic.

Life in the Arctic

What did you learn about life in the Arctic?

1 Why is it hard to live in the Arctic?

2 How do some Arctic animals change with the seasons?

3 How does blubber help animals?

4 What is your favorite Arctic animal? Why?

5 How has life changed for people in the Arctic?